BRUEGHEL

A GIFT FOR TELLING STORIES

CONTENTS

Painting on cover: *Peasant Wedding Feast* (about 1567), detail.

Graphic design: Sandra Brys

First published in the United States in 1995 by Chelsea House Publishers.

© 1993 by Casterman, Tournai

First Printing

1 3 5 7 9 8 6 4 2

ISBN 0-7910-2806-2

ART FOR CHILDREN

BRUEGHEL

A GIFT FOR TELLING STORIES

By Pierre Sterckx

Illustrations by Claudine Roucha

Translation by John Goodman

CHELSEA HOUSE PUBLISHERS

NEW YORK • PHILADELPHIA

CHILDREN'S GAMES

he story begins in Brussels, in one of the narrow streets leading to the Grand Sablon, an old town square. This neighborhood is full of antique stores, cafés, and restaurants. It's easy to spend hours here window shopping, looking at the statues on the old guild buildings, or playing in the park. But the small blond girl with chestnut eyes was not interested in cookies or old pictures. She was watching a boy her own age, about 10 years old, who was absorbed in an odd game.

"How strange!" she said, watching a sort of wooden pear spin on its iron tip.

The boy hit it with a long string, which made it move faster. It headed down the street, jumping from cobblestone to cobblestone. Close up you could hear it whirr.

A shop window full of good things to eat.

"What's the name of that thing?" said the little girl.

"What's your name?" asked the boy, turning away from his toy for a moment.

"Gabriella."

Then it fell off its tip and started twisting every which way. The boy picked it up and stroked it absent-mindedly.

"I've never seen one of these," said the little girl, examining the object. "Where I come from we don't play with them."

"No one does anymore; it's an old toy. My grandfather gave it to me. It's a klachdop."

"A what?"

"A top that you hit. You don't know the Brussels dialect?"

"I come from Italy, from Rome. My mother is Italian and my father is Belgian; he's a doctor."

"Gabriella!" a woman cried.

"Yes, mother, I'm coming."

The two children went into a small, dark shop full of old furniture, copper kettles, dusty books, wooden toys, cut glass, and many other mysterious objects that they could not identify in the gloom. Gabriella's mother spoke with an elderly man. She was holding an old piece of earthenware that must have held gallons of beer in the course of its long life.

"Look!" cried Gabriella, examining the cover of a large book on a pile of old tomes. "They're playing with your top!"

"Gosh, you're right!" said the little boy.

"Oh!" gasped Gabriella, looking at a detail in the picture of a little girl playing with a stick on a pile of mud that might well be something a lot dirtier. But she was only pretending to be upset; in fact, she thought the book's cover was won-

Children's Games (1560).

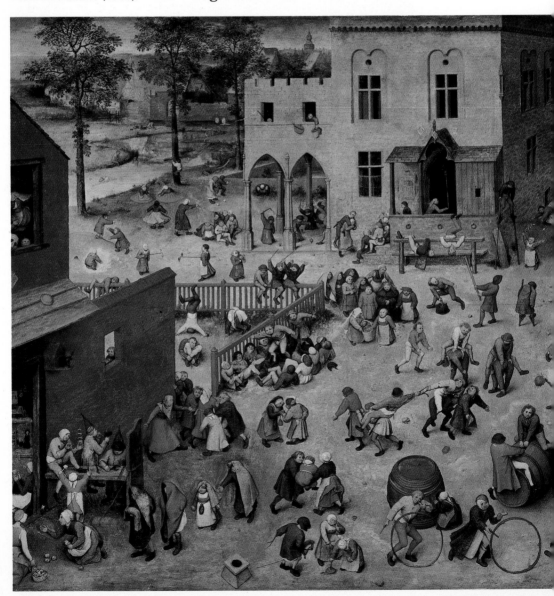

Sablon Square is surrounded by handsome 17th-century houses.

derful. It showed hundreds of children in the center of an old town playing all kinds of games in small groups of two to five.

The little boy proudly identified the old games. "That one is blind-man's bluff. Farther up they're throwing balls into a hole. There are stilts as well as hoops, and pig bladders being blown up like balloons, and barrels. And those two are making a seat for a little girl."

"I see some who are pulling a little boy's hair, and others who are about to drop a fellow onto a beam," said Gabriella. "They weren't very nice back then. Why does this one carry a knife in his mouth?"

"Because he failed to throw it at the ground so it would stick straight up; that's his punishment."

"It's beautiful, isn't it?" said the old gentleman with a smile. "All those kids playing seem like red and blue ants scurrying every which way. As though a giant had stepped on their nest. Pieter Brueghel, who painted this picture, had quite an imagination."

"Isn't his house nearby, Grandfather?" asked the boy.

"Yes, Vincent," said the old man. "It's at the corner of the rue Haute, and his tomb is in Our Lady of the Chapel church, which is also nearby. You should go and see it."

"And his painting in the museum!" added Vincent. "Can we go and see that, too?"

"He's your greatest painter," said Gabriella's mother.

"Absolutely, the greatest of all, and for a simple reason: he dealt with the people, with science, and with the earth!"

"How much is this book?"

"I'll throw it in if you buy the jug."

A current map of the Marolles quarter in which Brueghel lived.

Gabriella and her mother spent that evening looking at the book in their beautiful apartment, whose turn-of-the-century windows look out on the chestnut trees in 50th Anniversary Park. The mother often said that Brussels was a great city—beautiful and very affordable. Although it's much smaller than Rome, Paris, or London, it has everything one needs to live well, from the best chocolate to high quality opera.

On a low table sat the large earthenware jug, brown and shiny. It now held a bouquet of white lilacs. Unfortunately its handle was broken.

"But it's still beautiful, isn't it, mother?"

The 50th Anniversary Park in Brussels contains the Royal Museums of Art and History.

"**L**et's take stock of where we are," said Gabriella to herself, closing her eyes and pulling the bedcovers over her chin. Her little head was full of the events of the remarkable day. "To sum up," she continued, "Brueghel's life as an artist began in Antwerp. We know the date of his entry into the painter's guild there. He took this step in 1551. But we know nothing of his earlier life. Neither the date nor the place of his birth are mentioned in the local archives. He might have been from Breda, in Holland, or from Bree, in Belgium. Given that 25 was the minimum age for guild membership, it is assumed that he was born in 1526."

"That's important," Gabriella said to herself, "for it enables us to determine his age when he died in 1569." Gabriella remembered the visit she and her mother had made that very afternoon to the church of Our Lady of the Chapel, at the end of the rue Haute. It is a pretty church with a slate bell tower that looks like a black hat. Gabriella looked for Brueghel's tomb there but saw only marble monuments with carved skeletons in memory of other people whose names she quickly forgot. There was no trace of the painter. The sacristan of the church, who happened by, had told them: "That's because in 1789 crazed French revolutionaries wrecked everything here. They even destroyed Brueghel's tomb."

"From 1526 to 1569, that's only 43 years!" Gabriella threw off the covers and sat up in her bed. "That's about my father's age!" she mumbled. "He died very young, this Pieter Brueghel."

So that was the meaning of the Latin phrase in the book: *medio aetatis suae*, died in the middle of his age. In an old engraving reproduced there, he appears in profile with a long beard and seems much older. But he was probably suffering from rheumatic fever at the time and also from a stomach ailment, perhaps an ulcer. In those days little could be done for such problems.

"There must be some mistake," she said to herself, leaning back a bit. "How could he have made so many marvellous things in so short a time? All these mysteries: place and date of birth unknown, his tomb gone, and about 50 masterpieces thought up and executed between the ages of thirty and forty."

Painter and the Art
er (ca. 1565).

If it is true that Brueghel worked exclusively in drawing and print media between 1544 and 1559 and that in this same period he traveled in Italy, spending time in Rome and then Sicily and Naples, only some 10 or 11 years remain in which he could have completed his remarkable body of painted work!

Presumed portrait of Brueghel, detail from *The Peasant Wedding Feast.*

The Fall of the Rebel Angels (1562).

"I have to tell Dad about all this," she said to herself. "He'll be interested." And she reviewed one last time this short history of Pieter Brueghel the elder (not to be confused with his son, known as the younger), remembering something that Vincent's grandfather had told them: "The story goes that Brueghel died trying to look at Brussels upside down. He stood on his head with his feet high up against a wall and died after having said: 'How beautiful it looks like that!'"

"Is that what people say?" Gabriella's mother had answered with a smile, half mocking and half amused, for she had studied art history in Rome before her marriage brought her to Brussels, where her husband was completing his medical studies.

"Yes," the shop owner had added. "I sometimes prefer what people tell me directly to what others take to be proven."

"I'm going back to Italy," Gabriella said to herself, knowing full well that this was a silly idea. But soon she was climbing a rocky mountain, making her way through an increasingly dark pass. She was very much afraid. Soldiers were pursuing her. Stopping for a moment, she thought she could hear their horses. Suddenly a fat, puffy gnome appeared sitting beside the path. He was blind and had a noisy laugh. Gabriella wanted to ask for directions but instead found herself saying to him, "Do you know any good proverbs?" "A stitch in time saves nine," said the little creature, running along the edge of a cliff while it started to snow heavily. The soldiers arrived; they took no notice of Gabriella but repeatedly stabbed the gnome's belly with their long swords, speaking Spanish and German all the while, and then continued on their way. Gabriella woke up with a start.

he Brussels art museum has columns and bronze sculpture on its facade; like most such places, it resembles an old court-house or at least a building where serious business is transacted. To reach the Brueghel room on the second floor, you have to pass through a large white entry hall containing marble sculpture and climb a stone stairway, keeping an eye out for signs that say: "16th and 17th centuries." Gabriella and her mother admired dozens of madonnas, crucifixions, tortured saints, and other such early Flemish themes, but they didn't stop. "When one has an appointment with a masterpiece in a museum," her mother said, "it's better to be on time."

They knew that they had arrived at the room they were seeking when they saw

a large panel bearing the name:
BRUEGHEL.

"There aren't many," said Gabriella
quickly. "One, two, three, four, five."

"There's another one in another
room," said her mother after looking at
the museum guide.

"Why are there so few, when we're in
his country, and even his city?"

"Belgium is a small country, Gabriella,
and it was often invaded in past centuries. In addition, Brueghel's best paintings left Antwerp shortly after his death.
They belonged to a rich businessman
from there, a Mr. Jonghelinck, who must
have turned them over to the authorities
because of tax problems."

"Like Uncle Mario?" asked Gabriella.

"No, much more serious!" cried her
mother, laughing and stroking her daughter's hair. "And then the city fathers
thought it might be a good idea to give
them to the sitting Austrian governor.
That's why Vienna now has the finest
collection of Brueghels in the world, no
less than 15 masterpieces!"

"We have to tell Dad to go and see
them!" said Gabriella, very excited.

"Yes, my dear, you can tell him over
the phone."

"I'd better warn you both that it will be
a long conversation."

Museum of Art in
sels.

"*The Fall of Icarus*," murmured Gabriella, looking at the painting, delighted at discovering it to be much larger, and its colors much softer, than in the book. "But I don't see anybody falling. Where's Icarus?"

"He's not easy to find," said her mother. "Look over there, behind the boat."

"It's a leg! A man's drowning! Is it Icarus, Mommy?"

"Yes, dear. He has fallen from the sky, from a great height."

"Hasn't he fallen off the ship?" asked Gabriella, who was a very practical and realistic girl.

"Look closely—do you see those small things in the air above the leg of poor Icarus?"

The Fall of Icarus (ca. 1555).

"They're white feathers," said Gabriella after a moment's reflection.

"Madame! Madame! Don't touch!" a voice cried.

The guard was annoyed. Museum visitors cannot get too close to old paintings since they are fragile. Even bright light can damage them.

"We're sorry," she said to the guard, stepping back slightly.

"Exactly, feathers," she continued. "And that's how we can tell it's of Icarus and his fall into the sea. Do you know why he fell? I'll tell you the story. Icarus was trapped with his father Daedalus in the center of a labyrinth, which is a complicated maze. To escape, Daedalus made wings for them by gluing together with beeswax the feathers of birds he'd caught. Then they used the wings to fly off into the blue sky, free at last! But Daedalus' son Icarus, mad with joy at his new capacity for flight, rose up so high, so close to the sun, despite all his father's warnings, that the wax holding his wings together melted under the heat of its rays. His wings fell away and he plunged into the sea, where he drowned."

"It's a good story," said Gabriella, looking at the painting, "but Brueghel doesn't include any of that, aside from the feathers and the sea."

ou go to see *The Fall
carus* in Brussels, you
l not have the same
blem as Gabriella—
painting is now
ibited under glass.

19

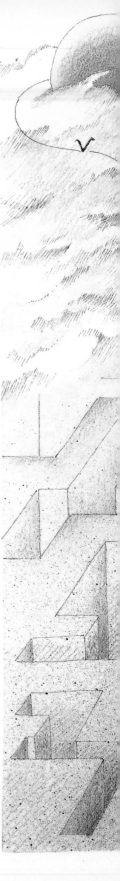

"That's true," said her mother. "Pieter Brueghel interpreted the Roman text of Ovid in a completely new way, a modern way. Do you see the ship with its majestic sails, and the man plowing a field? Everything shows the world of human beings in action, at work. Whether they engage in commerce, agriculture, or warfare, the fate of Icarus matters little to them: life goes on."

"Then what did Icarus represent for Brueghel?"

"A poet, a madman, a dreamer, I don't know for sure. What do you think?"

"Maybe an astronaut," said Gabriella. "Before the space shuttle, when they came back from the moon they always fell into the water."

And she went to look at the other paintings hanging in the large gray room, one on each wall.

Print of a seascape illustrating the fall of Icarus.

Yawning Man (undated).

"Ah, there you are," said Gabriella to Vincent and his grandfather as they came into the room

At first glance she had not recognized the grandfather, for he had combed his hair and put on a nice tie.

"We were in the Delporte room," he said, "where there's another Brueghel, a small one with children and birds in the snow."

"Come look at it!" said Vincent. "I'll show you how they caught birds with a stick and string."

"First I want to ask you something," Gabriella said to the grandfather. "Do you know who that is?"

They were close to a small oval painting of the head of a man in a white shirt who was yawning, his mouth wide open and his eyes closed.

"He's a peasant, you can tell from his shirt and above all his sunburned cheeks. Brueghel really liked peasants. He observed and drew them often, working in the fields as well as during their celebrations and banquets. He painted himself into *The Peasant Wedding Feast*, now in Vienna. There's even a story that old Pieter and his friend Hans Franckert disguised themselves as peasants and offered gifts to the couple to get invited to the wedding!"

Hunters in the Snow (1565).

"That's interesting, but you haven't told me who this one was and where he was from."

"We'll never know," said the grandfather, "because he was a mere peasant. In those days, only nobles had any claim on being remembered."

"He's yawning because he's bored," said Vincent. "Just like me at school."

"And what do you think of the oval format?" her mother asked. "It's a bit unusual, isn't it?"

"Not really," murmured the grandfather. "The real answer to your question is in the Mayer Museum in Antwerp. Go see the *Twelve Proverbs* there and you'll see what I mean."

"When can we go?" asked Gabriella, who was still looking at the yawning man, much to Vincent's annoyance.

Peasant Wedding Feast (about 1567).

In the train taking them to Antwerp, Gabriella and her mother watched the flat landscape of Brueghel's country passing by. They saw a gray and overcast sky, windblown leaves, occasional breaks in the clouds, poplars lining the roads and canals, and church steeples in the distance.

The Brussels-Malines-Antwerp railway line was one of Europe's first; it opened around 1830. It made a strong impression on the author Victor Hugo, who wrote about it.

"Brueghel's century inherited some important inventions that changed the face of the world," said Gabriella's mother. "Between 1472 and 1519, for example, Leonardo da Vinci made some remarkable inverntions, including the centrifugal pump, the dredging machines used to dig canals, rifled gun barrels, the submarine, and machines for winding silk; and Alberti wrote the first treatise on perspective in 1440. How would Brueghel have been able to orchestrate his vast landscapes full of people and stories without the lessons of Italian art?

"But perhaps the most important of these inventions was the modern printing press devised by Gutenberg, also in 1440. Antwerp was home to one of the great printers of the 16th century: Plantin. We can visit his house, if we have time. And then there's Hieronymus Cock. He was a publisher of prints and illustrated books whose shop was called 'To the Four Winds,' a motto intended to signal his international ambitions."

The Chinese had used movable type since A.D. 1,000, but Gutenberg was the first to standardize the process, manufacturing interchangeable characters that could be widely used. In the course of a few decades, the books and pamphlets produced using his type transformed written communication, making the hand-written manuscript almost obsolete. Some of young Brueghel's patrons in Antwerp were involved in the production of printed images.

Gutenberg, copper-plate engraving, Paris (1584).

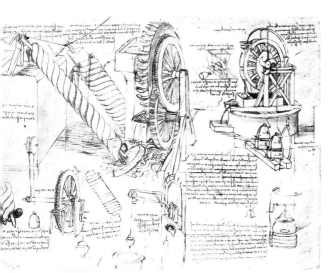

Plantin's house in Antwerp is now home to a museum of printing and publishing.

Leonardo da Vinci. *Studies of suction-pumps.* Pen and ink. Codex Atlanticus.

During Brueghel's lifetime great advances were made in science and technology. In 1545 Ambroise Pare first performed what was to become modern surgery; the first astronomical map dates from 1539; our present alegbraic symbols were invented by Stifel in 1544; and agriculture benefited from the invention of the wheeled plough, which made deeper furrows possible (one of these is visible in *The Fall of Icarus*). From 1550 on, three-masted seafaring ships—painted and drawn so well by Brueghel—were capable of heading into the wind, making Atlantic crossings less difficult, and ways of manufacturing window glass and lenses for glasses were developed. Seeing clearly, reading a great deal, and traveling rapidly became the underpinnings of the new culture.

The Painter and the Art Lover (detail).

The anguish that is so evident· in several paintings by Brueghel the elder and his insistence on painting madness, disasters, death, violence, and loss leads us to suppose that the painter must have witnessed tragic events, or at least had very good reason to fear that such events might come to pass.

As ·a result, Brueghel had a deep interest in the work of the painter Hieronymus Bosch. Another reason for this interest was that his patron Hieronymus Cock deeply admired him and asked Brueghel to draw or engrave several illustrations in Bosch's fantastic style. In fact, Bosch had already sensed that ·the structure of medieval society, built over the preceding five centuries, was in the process of collapsing. In his *Fall of the Rebel Angels*, Brueghel painted his own vision of nature gone mad, a theme that had obsessed Bosch.

The Hay Wain, Hieronymus Bosch.

It could be argued that most of the misfortunes of the modern world resulted from a single invention —firearms, especially cannons. In the 14th century, a mere hundred years before Brueghel's birth, these terrible objects were still not very dangerous and had not yet greatly increased the destructive power available to princes, kings, and their armies. But after a certain point they evolved with astonishing speed. Already in 1471 iron musket and cannonballs were invented, and the growing power of firearms increased their range. Cannons and other firearms dominated the field of battle, decimating cavalry, rendering protective armor useless, and making many fortified strongholds newly vulnerable.

Two engravings that are similar to Brueghal's work.

In Brueghel's paintings there are many damaged towers, houses, and fortresses, as well as burning cities. The growing power of artillery transformed not only warfare but international politics. The demand for firearms grew especially quickly at the beginning of the 16th century. From that point on, no ruler could imagine conquering territories or even safeguarding his authority without an army equipped with cannons.

The production of artillery required iron. Consequently, mines were dug to search for this metal, trees were cut down to provide supports for the tunnels, and larger and larger enterprises were developed which called for large amounts of money. This was the beginning of what is called capitalism (from the word *capital,* which means investment money provided by an absent owner who provides the tools and profits from the labor of the workers). It was also the beginning of what rapidly became colonialism: the kings of Spain and Portugal sent fleets of ships to conquer South America, and other monarchs soon followed their example. Gold and more gold was needed to pay for the new military machine. It was in 1541 (when Brueghel was probably a teenageer) that Pizarro and 182 men equipped with muskets defeated the Inca emperor Atahualpa. The Peruvian Indians were almost exterminated in the course of the next 30 years, perishing in gold mines, where they were worked to death.

Method for Collecting Gold from Appalachian River Beds, print by Theodore de Bry (1563) from the *Brevis Narratio.*

In Antwerp there's a zoo and a river, two attractions that greatly interested Gabriella. But her curiosity about Pieter Brueghel the elder and her desire to know more about the small yawning peasant made her resist going to see the bears and lions strutting in the sun and the boats lined up at the docks. Both mother and daughter liked to walk, so they avoided the bright red cable cars and went directly to the Mayer van den Bergh Museum on foot. It took them twenty minutes to get there from the train station. They strolled down the Meier, which is Antwerp's main commercial street, until they reached the Boeren Toren, a skyscraper built by farmers' organizations that was designed to rival the splendid tower of the nearby Gothic cathedral. And there on the left, beyond a

walkway lined with clothing stores, tea rooms, and antique shops (which greatly tempted Gabriella's mother), was the museum with its two precious Brueghels.

"But it's so small!" exclaimed Gabriella on seeing the facade of the handsome, gabled sixteenth-century residence built of brick.

The inside didn't resemble a museum so much as the sumptuous interior of an old Antwerp house full of furniture, tapestries, and paintings from the Gothic and Baroque periods. There were marvels in every oak-paneled corner. This Mr. Fritz Mayer van den Bergh was a rich art lover who lived in the last century. He did not want to study or become too involved in the business of the family, which had acquired an enormous fortune selling spices and medicine, as well as from beer-making and overseas shipping. He died at a relatively young age in 1901. His only passion was for acquiring works of art. Everything in this Antwerp house, which was built as a memorial by his mother, was in his personal collection, which he had left to the city of Antwerp when he died.

"It's wonderful," the little girl said politely, "but where are the Brueghels?"

"On the second floor," her mother answered. "Let's look at these other things first."

Gabriella was amazed by a work by master artist Heinrich von Kostanz, a lifesize piece in painted wood from the early forteenth century depicting Saint John falling asleep on the shoulder of Jesus, who holds his hand. Everyone who sees this work falls silent, and legend has it that when the sculptor had completed this masterpiece even he was stunned.

Heinrich von Kostanz. *Christ and Saint John,* painted walnut, about 1300.

Finally they found themselves in front of the two paintings by Brueghel, which were hanging on the same wall in a large front room. The light there was good, and they could see every detail. The title of the larger one is *Dulle Griet*, which means Mad Meg. It shows a large thin woman in helmet and breast plate, carrying a sword in one hand and booty in the other and marching through a devastated landscape.

Children's Games (detail).

"Look at the sky! It's on fire!" murmured the mother. "How brilliantly the reds and oranges are blended together! You know, Brueghel was the first Flemish painter to have painted things like fire and water, like wind, movement, and clouds, so fluidly. But he still used the old techniques and materials. *Dulle Griet*, for example, is painted on an oak panel made of planks held together by pegs. After building the panel Brueghel covered it with a white paste made of plaster and chalk, which he used to polish the wood until it was as smooth as a mirror. That's what gives the painting its inner glow."

"What a lot of work! It must have taken a lot of time!"

"He had young assistants. Do you remember that in his painting *Children's Games* there were children crushing bricks into powder? Why do you suppose they did that?"

"To make paint!" Gabriella immediately replied.

"Exactly. He made his paints himself from rocks and minerals."

Gabriella was fascinated by details of the painting that both frightened and amused her. At the bottom there was a sort of balloon man dangling a fish on a rod over a cracked egg full of chicks. And

Dulle Griet (detail).

also a strange fellow walking about with his head down, though his head was also his body and his mouth was also his rear end; a spoon stuck out of it, and he was trying to eat from a dish.

"The world turned upside down," said the little girl. "It's like that story about Brueghel looking at the landscape upside down."

"Yes. Meg has gone mad because of all the war, fire, killing, and pillaging around her. Do you see the harp sticking out of an egg? It's being played by a spider!"

"He's playing his web!" said Gabriella, laughing.

Dulle Griet (1562).

But she was already examining the other painting, with its twelve proverbs, each painted inside the hollow of a wooden plate. Each of the round images illustrated a text in Flemish that appeared underneath it. Gabriella leaned over so far to read them that she would have fallen over if her mother hadn't caught her. Here is what she read under the last image: "What ick vervol ghe, en geraecke daar niet aen-ick pisse altyt tegen de maen." Neither Gabriella nor her mother understood a word of this, for it was old Flemish and they didn't know very many words even in modern Flemish.

"We'll write it down and then ask Vincent's grandfather to translate it for us."

"Very good, and we'll ask him what my yawning man has to do with the fellow giving flowers to pigs, or the one knocking his head against a wall, or the one tying a bell around a cat's neck. Does any of this make sense to you, mother?"

Here are the Flemish proverbs that Gabriella copied at the Mayer van den Bergh Museum in Antwerp (from left to right)

* Drinking continually, even after one is already drunk, leads to poverty, dishonor, and ruin. * I am such an opportunist that I always turn my coat to catch the wind, whichever way it is blowing. * Fire in one hand, water in the other, I spend my time with gossips and idle women (or: The wicked sow discord). * No one feasted like I did, but now, reduced to misery, I'm between two chairs, sitting in ashes. * The calf looks askance at me, what's the point of covering the well now that it has drowned? (or: Remorse after the fact serves no purpose). * If you want do something useless, scatter roses to pigs (or: Do good to those who are worthy). * Armor makes me a spirited fighter and I tie a bell around the cat (or: Armor makes even cowards feel bold). * My neighbor's luck wracks my heart, I can't stand to see the sun reflected in the water (or: Envy is the enemy of happiness). * I am aggressive, violent, and irascible, so I beat my head against the wall (or: Anger is the cause of its own problems). * Fasting for me and feasting for others, it seems like I'm always fishing (or: He who is incapable strives in vain). * I wear a blue coat, but the more I hide myself the more easily recognizable I become (or: A wife's infidelity brings notoriety to the husband despite himself). * Whatever I desire, I never manage to obtain (or: Don't aim too high).

Twelve Proverbs (1558).

35

Fire in one hand, water
in the other, I spend my
time with gossips and
idle women.

I am such an opportunist
that I always turn my
coat to catch the wind,
whichever way it is
blowing.

nking continually,
n after one is already
nk, leads to poverty,
nonor, and ruin.

"You know, proverbs and stories always originate in popular wisdom. For example, the woman in the third painting of the top row carries a hot coal in one hand and a pail of water in the other, which means that one cannot keep going back and forth between fire and water—which is to say between good and evil, truth and falsehood—all one's life: eventually one has to choose. Unfortunately the meanings of proverbs are often lost over time, and as a result they can no longer influence people's bad behavior, like that of Mad Meg, for example."

"And Brueghel was on friendly terms with peasants," remembered Gabriella. "So it's not surprising that he loved proverbs."

"He was very aware of the injustices and misfortunes that are a part of life, but he was also an optimist who loved people."

"Was there a lot of misfortune in his time?" asked the dreamy little girl, looking once again at the fires in the painting of Mad Meg.

Trouble began in Flanders when Emperor Charles V of Spain abdicated in 1555 in favor of his son Philip II. Until then, Spanish troops were maintained in Flanders solely to fight against the king of France. But Philip II sent new regiments to crush his political opponents: Protestants, overly assertive and independent nobles, and the peasantry, who were sorely overtaxed. In 1555 the members of the Belgian Council of State asked to be allowed to take part in decisions pertaining to the Low Countries. Philip II did not respond, and in 1556 he made public his intention to repress heretics. In 1559 the king went even farther, appointing several inquisitors—judges charged with torturing heretics and burning them—as bishops in Flanders. While Charles V had done little more than prohibit the peasant festival gatherings known as kermises, Philip II's inquisitors burned a poor citizen of Antwerp at the stake for having written a song against the Franciscan order. Things went from bad to worse. The Protestants had allies in the nobility and among the people, and in 1566 they rebelled, smashing the "idolotrous" images in Catholic churches (such systematic destruction of images is known as iconoclasm).

Flemish 16th-century painting showing the Duke of Alva hearing the pleas of a group of chained women after repressive measures were enacted against the Protestant uprising.

The following year was marked by the arrival in Brussels of the Duke of Alva, sent by Philip II to subdue the revolt. An army of 60,000 Spanish soldiers supported the actions of a "Tribunal of Troubles," also called the "Council of Blood." The council put 8,000 people to death in less than two years (the population of Antwerp at this time was about 100,000). The public beheading of the Counts Egmond and Hoorn in 1569 and the imposition of more taxes the following year led to a general revolt. It was in the midst of this upheaval that Brueghel died, on September 5, 1569.

These tumultuous events are reflected in Brueghel's last paintings, especially *Magpie on the Gallows*, which shows peasants dancing at the foot of a gibbet, *The Triumph of Death*, a gigantic depiction of carnage at the hands of living skeletons, *Storm at Sea*, with its all-devouring whale, and *Massacre of the Innocents*, which drew a parallel between Herod's slaughter of first-born children and the recent vio-

***The Triumph of Death* (1562–1563)**

lence. All these paintings were executed in 1567 and 1568. And the artist's last work *The Misanthrope*, which shows a man distancing himself from society who is being robbed, suggests that at the end of his life Brueghel may have lost the optimism that had won him the nickname the Jolly Fellow.

Lamoral, the Count of Egmond

The Land of Cockaigne (1567)

The Spanish police never threatened Brueghel despite the fact that some of his paintings attacked the oppressors, for none of his works were openly hostile to the Spanish. Cardinal Granvella and other powerful individuals looked out for him and bought his paintings. He was even exempted from the general obligation to house and feed Spanish soldiers in his home on the rue Haute. Doubtless the mayor realized that it would be best to let Brueghel work in peace and that his remarkable paintings were more important than any civic obligation.

During the same two final years of his life Brueghel painted cheerful works such as *Peasant Wedding Feast, Peasant Kermis, The Peasant and the Nest Robber,* and *The Land of Cockaigne,* in which we see a boiled and cracked egg running toward a man who has already eaten so well that he has fallen into a deep sleep. Doubtless this illustrates the Flemish superstition that goblins take refuge in cooked eggs unless the eggs are completely eaten and their shells crushed.

THE TRUTH ABOUT THE
YAWNING MAN

"A ctual size," proclaimed Gabriella's father as he unrolled a reproduction more than three feet wide.

And Gabriella immediately recognized one of "her" painter's last paintings: *Storm at Sea*. On this scale it was easy to make out the details, especially the whale, its mouth wide open as it pursues a ship.

"It's going to be swallowed up," said Vincent, who was eyeing a box of pralines brought by his grandfather, which was now next to a rice custard that was being served by Gabriella's mother.

"No," said the grandfather, "look at the barrel between the monster and the ship. Brueghel is illustrating another proverb: 'Don't sink the boat for a barrel.' Or even: 'Don't chase two hares at once.' Some people think this painting illustrates the story of Jonah. He was a prophet who was thrown from a ship. God sunk his ship in a storm, then sent a whale to swallow him up and spit him out un-harmed on the coast of the country where he was to preach the gospel."

"But," said Gabriella, "if the whale didn't digest Jonah, it didn't have anything to eat. Maybe it's yawning from hunger."

There was a general outcry at this point, for everyone knew that the main purpose of this Saturday afternoon tea party, in the beautiful sunny apartment facing the park, was not to celebrate a father's return home, nor to introduce an antique dealer to a doctor, nor to consume port, coffee, chocolates, and cake. All these things were secondary, as Gabriella had just managed to remind everyone. They were there to answer the burning question: Who was the little yawning peasant?

"If I may say something," said Gabriella's father, "even though I'm not a specialist, it seems to me that Gabriella's observation proves that this painting is indeed by Brueghel. The yawning man yawns, and so does the whale. Yawning was an action for which Brueghel had great affection."

"What, an art critic?" said Gabriella's mother. "My dear, I'd say you had a gift!"

Storm at Sea (1568). This painting was first attributed to Joos de Momper, but it was later thought to be Brueghel's because of its broad, fluid handling and thinly-applied pigments. A recent chemical analysis of its support has resulted in its being reattributed to de Momper.

Magpie on the Gallows
(1568).

Vincent said nothing; his mouth was full.

"But why paint the portrait of a simple peasant in those days? The question is worth asking," said the mother, looking at the old antique dealer, "and we didn't find an answer at the Mayer Museum in Antwerp."

"I have a suggestion," said the grandfather. "You saw the *Proverbs* painted on round wooden plates. Early on Brueghel drew and engraved not only a series of proverbs but also a set of vices and virtues. Perhaps this yawning man is not just the portrait of a fellow with bad manners who doesn't cover his mouth when he should."

"Don't look at me like that," said Vincent, wondering what flavor his next praline would be.

"Yawning is the illustration of a vice."

"Let's see," said Gabriella's father, "Maybe it's 'Speaking without saying anything'."

"Not bad," exclaimed the antique dealer. "Do you know why Brueghel placed a magpie on top of a gallows in one of his paintings? Some say it was because he wanted to see all idle chatterers hanged!"

"I'd say it was a picture of boredom," said his wife, "which is the beginning of all vices."

"And I think it's laziness," exclaimed Gabriella. "When you don't do anything for a long time, you yawn."

"That must be it," said the grandfather.

"And the other vices?" Vincent asked his grandfather.

"Lost, all lost; the paintings were so very small. All that remains is the lazy yawning man with crow's feet and a big black hole in the middle of his face."

"Yes, that's perfect!" everyone cried.

"Does that satisfy you, Gabriella?"

"I'd like some custard," she answered, with a smile that indicated she was indeed satisfied.

And Gabriella joined Vincent in illustrating gluttony.

It was at this moment that Dr. De Man (that was Gabriella's family name) decided to tell a story worthy of his medical expertise.

ust imagine," said Dr. De Man to his charming wife, "when I went to the museum in Vienna to see Gabriella's 19 Brueghels . . ."

"Fifteen," corrected Gabriella.

"I was accompanied by Guy Marlier."

"The optometrist?"

"Yes. And he told me a story that will interest you. Do you know the painting by Brueghel called *Parable of the Blind*?"

"Here it is," said Gabriella, opening her big book to the right page and placing it on the table in front of them.

"That's it," said the father. "A perfect picture for an eye doctor, don't you think? Do you know what it means?"

"That's easy," said Gabriella. "The blind men follow one another. In the end, they all fall into the river. It must be another proverb."

"It illustrates a verse from the gospel of Matthew," said Vincent's grandfather: " 'Can the blind lead the blind?' "

"Better yet," said Gabriella's mother, "Brueghel could be making fun of those who prefer believing to seeing. He might be arguing that Saint Thomas was right to want to see the risen Christ before believing in the miracle. And then," added Madame De Man, "what a fine study of accelerating movement this

painting is. To the left, two blind men are still firmly on their feet, and they use a horizontal pole to steady themselves. But the two figures in the center are beginning to stumble. One of them is on the verge of falling and seems to push a fifth blind man into the trench with his cane. As for the sixth one, he's already in the ditch. It could almost be an illustration of Galileo's theorem of accelerated motion on an inclined plane."

Parable of the Blind (1568).

"That's fascinating!" everyone cried in unison.

"Your mother is something else," said Vincent. "She knows almost as much as my grandfather."

"Why no," Gabriella kindly protested.

"What you've just argued, dear," said Gabriella's father after sipping a bit of port, "fits with what Marlier told me. These aren't generalized blind people. Marlier was able to diagnose every one of their problems: glaucoma, atrophied sockets, etc."

"So Brueghel must have made a very close study of individuals who couldn't see any more," said Vincent's grandfather.

"Exactly. Add that to the study of

accelerated motion toward a fall, so brilliantly evoked by my wife, and this painting becomes a remarkable tribute to the art of seeing. And there's more!"

"Really!" said the old antique dealer. "Brueghel had quite a gift for telling stories in pictures"

"Gabriella told me about the painter's death, which was probably caused by an internal hemmorage. We know that Brueghel had stomach problems. Now according to my optometrist friend, in the Middle Ages they believed that stomach illness made noxious vapors rise into the head that made you go blind."

"You're suggesting that Brueghel might have thought so, too?" asked Gabriella's mother.

"It seems likely. He might have made a close study, like a doctor, of the various ways one might go blind as a way of looking out for himself and perhaps to lessen his fear of losing his own sight. And he didn't die blind! He died looking at the world upside down."

The human body was carefully studied in this period. In 1543 a resident of Brussels named Vesalius published *De humani corporis fabrica libri septem*, an examination of human anatomy illustrated with engravings of remarkable scientific precision.

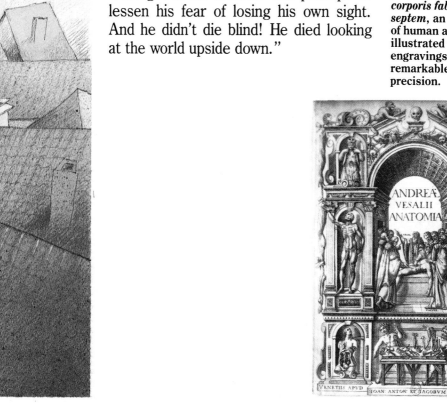

EATING WELL, BRUSSELS STYLE

"Tell me, grandfather, what did people eat in Brueghel's day?"

"In Brussels, like everywhere in Belgium, people have always eaten well. Can you think of another city where, as in Brussels, there are 120 streets named after food? There's even a Butter Street here! But there wasn't always enough to go around. So food became something of an obsession for most people. And on festival days they stuffed themselves. Pigs were roasted, sugared raisin bread was prepared, and there were waffles galore. That reminds me: I have to give your mother the Belgian recipes she asked for."

"Did they eat a lot of french fries?"

"No! Not at all. Potatoes didn't become standard fare in this region until much later. They ate mostly black bread and occasionally some vegetables and fish."

While explaining all this to Vincent and Gabriella, the grandfather was busy making waffle batter.

"Did they drink as much as they ate?" asked Gabriella.

"They drank all the time, because in those days meat and fish were preserved in salt. Some wine was brought by boat from France, but beer was already the principal beverage."

And the grandfather proceeded to sing the praises of the Belgian brews being made today.

"There," he finally said, "the batter is ready and the iron is hot, so let's get started."

"Are we going to serve them with sugar?" asked Vincent.

"Or with butter or with ice cream—I even have a few strawberries—or with cherry jam . . ."

"Can I please have one with butter, sugar, ice cream, and strawberries?"

"No, Vincent, that would be too much."

Belgian Waffles

2 cups flour, 3 teaspoons baking powder, ½ teaspoon salt, 3 separated eggs, 1¾ cups milk, 4 tablespoons melted butter, 3 tablespoons sugar.

Combine the flour, baking powder, and salt in a bowl. In a separate bowl beat the egg yolk well and add the milk and butter. Combine the flour and yolk mixture and beat until smooth. Beat the egg whites until stiff, but not dry. Slowly add the sugar, beating constantly. Mix a third of the beaten whites gently into the batter, then fold in the remaining whites very carefully. Spread ½ cup of waffle batter in the hot waffle iron. Bake until golden.

Bon appetit.

MY FAVORITE BRUEGHEL

"All things considered, what's your favorite painting by Brueghel?" asked Vincent's grandfather of the assembly.

"The *Yawning Man* in Brussels," said Gabriella without a moment's hesitation.

"Me, too," Vincent added, "I vote for Lazy Louis!"

But he only said this to please Gabriella, for the painting he really prefered was *The Land of Cockaigne*, with its sausage fences, pies on rooftops, and running boiled egg.

"My favorite is still *The Fall of Icarus*," said Gabriella's mother. "I love its soft colors. And you?"

"It's hard to choose," said the old man. "But in the end I'd pick *The Wheat Harvest* in the Metropolitan Museum in New

Peasant Kermis (1568–1569).

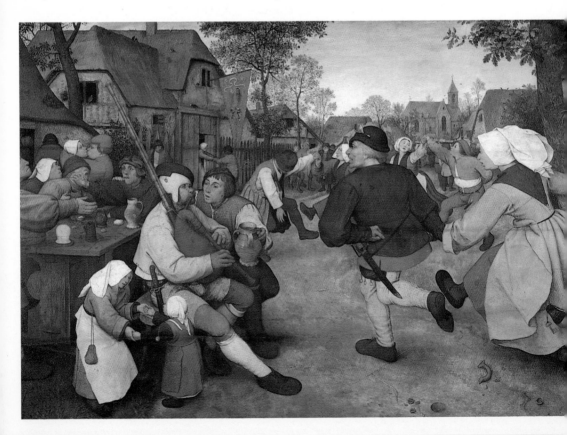

York, with its shoulder-high fields of golden wheat and its peasants lunching in the shade of a tree."

"As for me," said Gabriella's father, "I'd choose a picture in Vienna that we haven't even mentioned: *Peasant Kermis*, which represents a peasant festival. It's reproduced in the book. I like the size of the figures."

"It's true," said Madame De Man, "here Brueghel has completely abandoned his early taste for small figures and tiny details, as in *Children's Games*."

"The painting is very mysterious, if you look carefully," her husband continued. "Look at the figures on the left. There's a group of blind people sitting around a table who seem to be pledging some kind of oath. Behind them, a couple dressed in red are kissing each other on the mouth. In the foreground, a youngster teaches a child to dance. A bagpiper blows hard on his instrument, but there's almost no air in it. And the young man beside him looks like a complete idiot."

"That makes sense," said his wife, "the sound of bagpipes drives me crazy, too."

"But I think in this case we're dealing with a real idiot," said the grandfather, "because of the jug he's holding."

"What about this jug?" asked Gabriella.

"It has three handles," observed Vincent. "That's a lot for a jug."

53

"In fact it has four," said the grandfather. "The fourth one on the back isn't visible. So it's probably an 'idiot's jug,' which was invented at about this time."

"What are you saying, Monsieur Martelaere?" (That was the name of Vincent's grandfather—now you know it, just as our story comes to its close.) "Please explain yourself," said Gabriella's mother.

"Would you have a decent beer on hand, my dear lady?"

And when Monsieur Martelaere had consumed his beer, by which time everybody was impatient to hear his explanation (a situation that delighted him), he said:

"In those days, when Brueghel was young, the Emperor Charles V was hunting on the outskirts of Brussels, in the beautiful Soignes forest. In the late afternoon he found himself near a town called

A typical Brussels café.

Beersel. There, in an inn, he ordered a cold beer."

"Like you, grandfather?"

"Yes, except that the beer didn't over-flow the glass in which it was so kindly served to me."

"His beer overflowed a lot?" asked Gabriella.

"It overflowed onto the cuffs of his sleeves, which were made of sumptuous Bruges lace. The innkeeper had served him from his only jug, which had no handles, so the emperor was obliged to grip directly on its body with his hands. 'Innkeeper,' he said, 'next time I come be sure to have a jug with two handles.' His distinguished guest returned to the inn six months later, and this time the innkeeper appeared with a two-handled jug. But he stupidly gave it to the emperor gripping both handles himself, and once again the imperial sleeves were soaked with beer. The emperor ordered a three-handled jug made for him."

"It's a good thing this idiotic innkeeper didn't have three hands," said Vincent.

"No, but the next time he was dense enough to serve the jug such that the third handle was on his side rather than the emperor's. The exasperated ruler ordered a four-handled vessel made for him, and this type became known as a 'jughead's jug'."

Beersel Castle is a remarkable 14th-century fortress.

"And the broken handle in the painting?" said Gabriella.

"Where?"

"On the ground to the right, under the feet of the peasants beginning to dance."

"I hadn't noticed it," said Dr. De Man.

"Me either," said the grandfather.

"Bravo, Gabriella," whispered her mother.

"I know where it came from," said Gabriella, pointing to the piece of pottery they'd bought from Monsieur Martelaere a few weeks earlier, at a low price because it was flawed. "Maybe it's the handle that's missing from our jug!"

"No, Gabriella, that would be impossible! This jug was made in the 19th century, and Brueghel lived in the 16th century," the grandfather said.

"That's a difference of only three centuries," murmured Vincent.

"You know, you have a point; that isn't such a very long time," said the old antique dealer. "I'm your grandfather, and I was born in 1910. We're now in 1994. My own grandfather must have been born about 80 years earlier, say in 1830. My great grandfather would bring us back to around 1750. And my great great grandfather must have come into the world about 1670. Which means that my great great great grandfather was probably born around 1590, which is only some 20 years after Brueghel's death. In other words, its not such a long time, but enough to encompass a great deal of history, and a great many individual lives."

"That doesn't seem to interest you very much, Gabriella."

"Oh no, it does," she said, "but I'm trying to figure out how many grandfathers and great grandfathers I'd need to take me back to the age of the dinosaurs."

"That was more than 100 million years ago," said her father. "We'll figure that out another time."

GLOSSARY

atrophy: The decrease in size or wasting away of a body part.

Baroque: An artistic style popular in the 17th century marked by extravagant form and grotesque ornamentation.

Flanders: An area of Europe comprising what is now western Belgium and northern France.

Flemish: Of or relating to Flanders; a Dutch language spoken in Flanders.

glaucoma: A disease of the eye marked by increasing pressure in the eyeball that can damage the eye and lead to blindness.

The Notre Dame cathedral in Sablon, Brussels.

A labyrinth in the Van Buuren gardens, Brussels.

An art nouveau doorway in Brussels.

The Plantin museum in Antwerp.

Middelheim Park, Antwerp.

Gothic: An architectural style popular from the 12th to the 16th centuries marked by pointed arches and vaulting.

guild: A medieval assocation of craftmen or merchants that often regulated working conditions and set prices.

Low Countries: A region in western Europe comprising modern Belguim, Luxembourg, and the Netherlands.

optometrist: A doctor who specializes in treating eye disorders with excercises and corrective lenses.

Ovid: A Roman poet, ca. 43 B.C.–A.D. 17, who wrote down a number of myths, including the story of Icarus and Dedalus.

patron: A wealthy supporter of an artist.

perspective: The appearance to the eye of objects in respect to their relative distance and position.

proverb: A brief saying that usually reflects popular wisdom.

tome: A large or scholarly book.

Where are the works by Pieter Brueghel?

Photographic Credits